GOATS

by Liza Jacobs

BLACKBIRCH®
PRESS

THOMSON

GALE

San Diego • Detroit • New York • San Francisco • Cleveland • New Haven, Conn. • Waterville, Maine • London • Munich

THOMSON

GALE

For more information, contact
The Gale Group, Inc.
27500 Drake Rd.
Farmington Hills, MI 48331-3535
Or you can visit our Internet site at http://www.gale.com

Photographs © 1999 by Chang Yi-Wen

Cover photograph © PhotoDisc

© 1999 by Chin-Chin Publications Ltd.

No. 274-1, Sec.1 Ho-Ping E. Rd., Taipei, Taiwan, R.O.C.
Tel: 886-2-2363-3486 Fax: 886-2-2363-6081

LIBRARY OF CONGRESS CATALOGING-IN-PUBLICATION DATA

Jacobs, Liza.
  Goats / by Liza Jacobs.
      v. cm. -- (Wild wild world)
  Includes bibliographical references and index.
  Contents: Goats are mammals -- Goats are plant-eaters -- Baby goats are called kids -- Many kinds of goats.
   ISBN 1-4103-0075-7 (alk. paper)
   1. Capra--Juvenile literature. 2. Goats--Juvenile literature. [1. Goats.] I. Title. II. Series.

  QL737.U53J343 2003
   599.64'8--dc21   2003002548

Printed in Taiwan
10 9 8 7 6 5 4 3 2 1

Table of Contents

About Goats

Goats are mammals. There are wild goats and domestic goats. Domestic goats are animals raised to live alongside people. They a[r]e often raised for their meat or milk. People drink goat milk and use [it] to make butter and cheese. Domestic goats are kept as pets, too.

Goats have horns and short tails. They can balance easily on steep cliffs and ledges. A goat's strong legs and hooves help it cling to rocky surfaces. Each hoof is split and there is an opening in the middle. A soft part in the opening helps keep the goat from slipping. It also cushions their landing when they jump. Goats can leap from one rocky spot to the next without falling!

Eating Food

Goats are plant-eaters. They like to munch on leaves and grasse
Goats have no front teeth in their upper jaw. The sharp front
teeth in their lower jaw are made for pulling off rough plant
material. Goats use their strong back teeth to crunch up their
food. They also have tough skin inside their mouths. This protec
them from the scratchy or thorny parts of the plants they eat.

Plant foods are made of tough fibers that are hard to digest.
Goats have special stomachs to help them digest their food.
When goats eat, they chew and swallow quickly. One part of
their stomach, the rumen, helps break down the food. This
partly chewed food is then brought back up and chewed
again. This is called chewing cud. After the cud is swallowed,
it can be fully digested.

7

Wanderers

In the wild, goats wander from place to place. They are most active in the morning and late afternoon as they search for food and water.

Goats often travel in groups called herds. They mark areas where they walk by peeing and rubbing their heads against trees or rocks. This leaves their scent behind. It's an "I've been here" message to other animals. Goats rest during other parts of the day. They often find cool shady spots among the rocks.

Goat Babies

Baby goats are called kids. Most kids can jump soon after they are born. They quickly find other kids to play with. Kids often wrestle and play fight. This prepares them for being adults.

Adult males are called bucks. Bucks butt heads with each other to compete for a female during mating season. Before charging, a buck gets up on its hind legs to show that it is about to strike.

Kids Grow Up

A female goat is called a doe. Does usually give birth to one or two kids. Kids are not born with full-grown horns. As a kid grows, so do its horns.

Mothers stay close to their kids when they are young. Kids drink their mother's milk, or nurse, for 10 to 12 weeks.

The Bovine Family

Goats belong to a larger group of animals called bovines. Sheep, cattle, antelopes, and buffalo also make up this group. All bovines have horns, but there are many different kinds. Some are hollow, while others are solid. Some grow straight, while others twist and curve. Some are covered with skin and others are not.

⑥

⑦

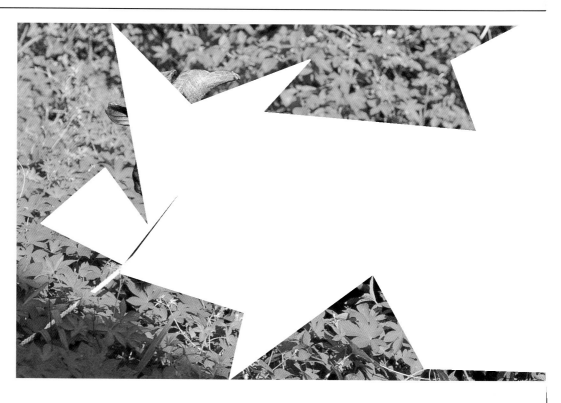

There are white,
off-white, brown,
reddish brown, and
black goats. There are
also goats with different
patterns of coat colors
and speckled markings.

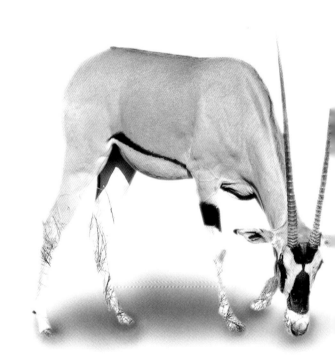

Different Kinds of Goats

There are many different kinds of goats—both wild and domestic. They are found in a wide range of coats and colors. Some goats have very short hair all over. Others have shorter hair on the front of their bodies and longer hair toward the back.

Some goats, such as angora goats, have long coats. Angora goats are raised for their soft fleece. The wool is used to make clothing and other items.

Horned Animals

Goats, sheep, cattle, and antelopes have hollow horns made out of the same material as fingernails. The horns cover bony growths on the head. Horns grow as an animal ages and it keeps its horns for life.

Deer have solid, bony antlers that often have many branches. They have a velvety outer covering. Deer shed, or drop, their antlers each year.

A rhinoceros has either one or two horns. Each one is completely solid. Giraffe horns are made of bone and covered with skin. They often feel soft to the touch.

Many of the animals shown on these pages have been hunted for their beautiful horns.

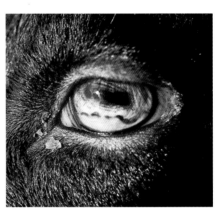

Sheep and Goats

Goats are closely related to sheep. Like goats, sheep tend to travel in groups. There are both wild sheep and domestic sheep.

There are, however, important differences between goats and sheep. Most sheep horns are twisted or curl forward and inward. Goat horns grow straight up, back, or out. Goats also have shorter tails than sheep.

 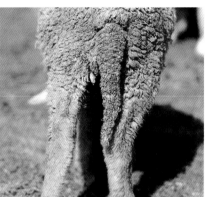

Goats and humans have developed a good relationship. Goats make good pets. On the farm, they can provide milk, fleece, and meat. All in all, a goat is a very useful animal!

For More Information

Arnold, Caroline. *Wild Goat.* New York: Morrow, 1990.

Miller, Heather. *My Goats (My Farm series).* Danbury, CT: Children' Press, 2000.

Miller, Sara Swan. *Goats (True Books: Animals series).* Danbury, CT: Children' Press, 2001.

Glossary

buck a male goat

doe a female goat

herd a group of goats

kid a baby goat

1

J
599.648   Jacobs, Liza.
J
Goats.

2120